American
Quakers

Edited and Introduced by
Wim Coleman

Quakers started many of the earliest schools for African American children.

Discovery Enterprises, Ltd.
Carlisle, Massachusetts

© Discovery Enterprises, Ltd., Carlisle, MA 1998

ISBN 1-57960-029-8 paperback edition
Library of Congress Catalog Card Number 97-68486

10   9   8   7   6   5   4   3   2   1

Printed in the United States of America

Subject Reference Guide:

American Quakers
Edited and Introduced by Wim Coleman

Society of Friends (Quakers) — U. S. History

Abolition of Slavery — U. S. History

Underground Railroad — U. S. History

William Penn — U. S. History

Women's Rights — U. S. History

Photos/Illustrations:

Cover art: *The Peaceable Kingdom* (1846) is the most famous painting by the primitive artist Edward Hicks, a Quaker preacher who lived in Philadelphia during the nineteenth century. There were sixty versions of this painting which Hicks named *The Peaceable Kingdom.*

Illustrations are from the Library of Congress,
except where otherwise noted in the text.

Table of Contents

Introduction:
Quaker Ways, Quaker Origins

by
Wim Coleman

Benjamin Franklin was a poor but ambitious teenager when he first arrived in Philadelphia early one Sunday morning in 1723. In his famous autobiography, he described something which happened shortly after his arrival.

Source: Benjamin Franklin, *Writings*, J. A. Leo Lemay, ed., New York: Library of America, 1987, p. 1329.

…I walked again up the Street, which by this time had many clean dress'd People in it who were all walking the same Way; I join'd them, and thereby was led into the great Meeting House of the Quakers near the Market. I sat down among them, and after looking round a while & hearing nothing said, being very drowzy thro' Labour & want of Rest the preceding Night, I fell fast asleep, and continu'd so till the Meeting broke up, when one was kind enough to rouse me. This was therefore the first House I was in or slept in, in Philadelphia.

Franklin's puzzlement upon his first experience in a Quaker silent meeting is typical, particularly of churchgoers accustomed to sermons, liturgy, hymns, and the like. Even today, such a meeting begins and ends in silence. If, during the course of the meeting, one feels moved "by the Spirit" or "out of the Light" to speak, one does so. Sometimes, several people may be so moved, with lively results. Other times, the congregation is quite content to spend the entire meeting in silence—

not an empty, hollow silence, but one which is as filled with the Spirit as any spoken testimony.

As Franklin discovered, this form of religious observance takes some getting used to. Indeed, it presents unique challenges to those who practice it. During the days of itinerant Quaker ministers, it sometimes led to awkward moments. A minister might be moved to travel hundreds of miles to a particular meeting, there to be greeted by Friends eager to hear his or her message. But during the meeting, the minister might be moved to say nothing at all! If so, it couldn't be helped. One could not prepare one's testimony, much less force it.

This form of worship is by no means the only thing which has separated Quakers from other people during their history. By the time Franklin showed up in Philadelphia, the Quakers were known, both in England and America, as a "peculiar people" with unique ideas about religion, behavior, and dress. How had they come by their startling practices and beliefs?

The founder of the Quakers was George Fox (1624-91), the son of a weaver in Leicestershire, England. By the time Fox was eleven years old, he was discontented with the religious beliefs and practices of those around him. As he saw it, people worshipped diligently on Sunday only to fail to carry their faith into everyday life. More disturbingly, the living Spirit of Christ was held at arm's length from ordinary churchgoers by a paid clergy. When Fox was nineteen, his discontentment reached a crisis. He left behind his job as a shoemaker and began wandering the country in search of nothing less than a new faith.

In a series of insights, visions, and revelations, Fox began to find this faith. He soon realized that churches (which he contemptuously called "steeple houses") and paid preachers were unnecessary for religious salvation. What mattered was a keen, intuitive attentiveness to "that of God in every one." Every single human being contained a divine spark, a glimmer of the Light of Christ. According to Fox, attention to one's own Inward Light was sufficient to inspire an ethical, moral, Christian life; attention to this Light in others was sufficient to produce a bond of communal love. The best way to find this Light was to simply sit in silence and wait. Such was the genesis of the Quaker silent meeting.

Fox soon began to acquire followers, variously known as "Children of Light," "Publishers of Truth," or "Friends of Truth." It has been said that they were first called "Quakers" because they sometimes trembled during their meetings. But Fox maintained that a magistrate named Gervase Bennett invented this nickname. In 1650, Fox was arrested in Derby, then charged by Bennett and another official with blasphemy. With characteristic bluntness, Fox advised his accusers to "tremble at the word of God." According to Fox, this admonishment prompted Bennett to call Fox's followers Quakers. It was only much later that the sect became known as the Religious Society of Friends, although individual Quakers were called "Friends" from a very early time.

In 1652, Fox had a vision which galvanized his determination to found a new faith. From that time on, he was the most implacable of prophets. For the sake of his flock, he needed to be, for England was not hospitable toward the new sect. The English Civil War had led to the execution of King Charles I and had put the Puritan Oliver Cromwell at the head of a new government known as the Commonwealth. Although Cromwell was somewhat sympathetic toward the Friends and genuinely fond of Fox, he could not prevent the sect from suffering terrible persecution at the hands of others, including his own followers.

This situation did not improve even after the restoration of the monarchy in 1660, despite the fact that King Charles II was also not ill-disposed toward the Quakers. During the eras of Cromwell and Charles, Quakers were variously mobbed, flogged, driven from their meeting houses (which were sometimes destroyed), and subjected to brutal imprisonment. Fox himself endured years of incarceration which took a permanent toll on his health. The persecution of the Friends did not wane until 1689, with the passage in Parliament of the Toleration Act. Friends occasionally suffered even after that.

Through all their early difficulties, the Quakers seldom compromised their ways or principles. In addition to holding illegal meetings of worship, they refused to pay tithes to the established Church. Moreover, they set themselves apart from other people by their plain and simple dress, their blunt and direct speech, and their seemingly uncivil behavior. When addressing others, even social superiors, they used the informal "thee" instead of the formal "you." The men refused to take off their hats even in the presence of royalty. And during their earliest days, they were infamous for disrupting "steeple-house" services with their own testimony.

They did not practice such standard church rituals as baptism or Holy Communion. To them, the essences of these concepts were inward and spiritual and could not be reduced to outward displays. They also refused to take oaths—in accordance, they insisted, with Christ's instructions: "But I say unto you, Swear not at all...But let your communication be, Yea, yea; Nay, nay: for whatsoever is more than these cometh of evil" (Matthew 5:31-7). After all, to live in the Light meant always to speak the truth—and of what possible meaning were oaths to Friends of Truth?

Because of their respect for all living human beings, the Quakers were also militant pacifists, refusing to take arms against others even in times of war. They generally refused to support warfare in any way, even by paying taxes or fees which might legally exempt them from military conscription. Friends' refusal to fight often put them at odds with the state, raising doubts as to their patriotism.

Surely no tenet stirred the suspicion and hostility of non-Quakers so much as the supremacy of the Inward Light in every human being. This ran contrary to established forms of Christianity, which insisted upon an intermediary between sinners and God in the form of a professional priesthood. To non-Quakers, such disregard for official religious hierarchy was truly alarming.

But the supremacy of the Inward Light posed a deeper problem than a denial of church authority. Of what importance was Holy Scripture in such a view? Could the Bible really be regarded as the inspired and infallible Word of God? George Fox himself revered the Bible greatly, and could quote from it so well that his severest critics sometimes wondered if he knew the book by heart. Fox held that the Bible was a vital part of a continual, unfolding revelation. This revelation was accessible to every living man and woman who sought it, as surely as it had been to Biblical prophets and apostles. Priests were not a vehicle toward this revelation, but an obstacle. As for the Bible, it could be a source of great comfort and inspiration when read in harmony with the Inward Light. But when read with slavish dogmatism, it could also be a spiritual stumbling block.

In an age when heresy was punishable by death, this was an extremely dangerous belief. It is rather amazing that the persecutions of the Quakers during the regimes of Cromwell and Charles II weren't worse than they were. Although some Friends perished under their afflictions in England, none were actually sentenced to execution.

Nevertheless, the English Quaker persecutions were very severe, and many Friends looked to other lands where they might find greater freedom. During the 1650s, some went to Ireland. Others went to Continental Europe and carried their ministry as far as Turkey. Still others turned toward a vast wilderness across the Atlantic—a land which had been known to Europeans for less than two centuries. A New World for a New Faith; what could make a better fit?

The Quakers in Colonial America

The first Friends to arrive in the New World were Mary Fisher and Ann Austin. They reached Barbados Island in 1655, then traveled to Boston in 1656. There they learned that New World Puritans were even less tolerant than Puritans in England. Their books were burned, and they were stripped and searched for signs of witchcraft. After five weeks of brutal imprisonment, they were sent back to Barbados.

Two days after Fisher and Austin left Boston, a ship with eight more Quakers arrived. They were imprisoned for eleven weeks, then shipped back to England. Laws were quickly passed against Quakerism. For a time, it seemed certain that the sect would never take root in America.

Then, in 1657, a leaky and barely seaworthy little vessel called the Woodhouse *sailed from England to America with eleven Quakers on board. These Friends went different ways in America, suffering terrible persecutions almost everywhere they went. Mary Clark was whipped, imprisoned, and banished from Boston. Christopher Holder and John Copeland were also whipped and incarcerated. Humphrey Norton was flogged and branded on the hand. Roger Hodgson was sentenced to hard labor, then flogged when he refused to work.*

As time went on, Friends in America suffered further brutalities. Some were branded or had their ears cropped; others were flogged from town to town; women were sometimes stripped naked. For a time, the only true safe haven in America for Quakers was Rhode Island, where Roger Williams had decreed complete religious freedom. Although Quakers often sought refuge there, they were too determined in their faith not to go where danger and persecution awaited them.

The Execution of Mary Dyer

In 1658, Massachusetts Governor John Endicott passed a law banishing all Friends from the colony on the pain of death. It wasn't long before four Friends received a call to defy this law. They were William Robinson, Marmaduke Stephenson, Mary Dyer, and the eleven-year-old Patience Scott, all of whom went to Boston.

The child was considered too young to be punished under the law, and was quietly sent home. Robinson, Stephenson, and Dyer were all officially banished by the General Court. They departed to Rhode Island, but in October, 1659, they returned to Boston, where they were sentenced to death. Robinson and Stephenson were hanged; Mary Dyer was reprieved on the scaffold and sent into banishment again.

Mary Dyer was pardoned on her first trip to the gallows, but she had to watch her two friends be hanged.

Not surprisingly, Dyer returned to Boston. Again, she was sentenced to death, and this time the sentence was ruthlessly carried out. English Friend Edward Burrough described her fate shortly after her execution.

Source: Hugh Barbour and Arthur O. Roberts, eds., *Early Quaker Writings: 1650-1700*, Grand Rapids, Michigan: Eerdmans, 1973, pp. 138-40. (Citation by Barbour and Roberts: Edward Burrough, *A Declaration of the Sad and Great Persecution and Martyrdom, 1660*. Unbracketed ellipses are in Barbour and Roberts' text; bracketed ellipses indicate a deletion on the part of the editor of this volume.)

Mary Dyer, being freed as aforesaid, returned to Rhode Island, and afterwards to Long Island, and there was most part of the winter, over the Island, where she had good service for the Lord; and then came to Shelter Island, whence she thought she might pass the Rhode Island. And being there, sometimes she had movings from the Lord to go to Boston, and there she came the 21st of the 3rd Month, 1660. And the 30th day was their Governor chosen, and the 31st of the 3rd Month, in the former part of the day, she was sent for to the General Court.

The Governor said, "Are ye the same Mary Dyer that was here before?"…

Mary Dyer: "I am the same Mary Dyer that was here the last General Court."

Then the Governor said, "You will own yourself a Quaker, will you not."

M.D.: "I own my self to be so reproachfully called." The bloody minded Jailer, having now opportunity to have his bloodthirsty will fufilled, said "she is a vagabond."

The Governor said, "The sentence was passed upon her the Last General Court, and now likewise: 'you must return to the prison from whence you came, and there remain until tomorrow at nine of the clock, then from thence you must go to the gallows, and there be hanged till you are dead.'"

Mary Dyer said, "this is no more than that thou saidst before."

"Aye, aye," the Governor said, "and now it is to be executed.

Therefore prepare yourself tomorrow at nine of the clock," (being the first day of the 4th Month, 1660).

Mary Dyer answered and said, "I came in obedience to the will of God, the last General Court, desiring you to repeal your unrighteous laws of banishment upon pain of death; and that same is my work now, and earnest request, because ye refused before to grant my request, although I told you that if ye refused to repeal them the Lord will send others of his servants to witness against them."

John Endicott asked her whether she was a prophet.

She said she spake the words that the Lord spake in her; "and now the thing is come to pass." She beginning to speak of her Call, J. Endicott said, "away with her, away with her."

So she was brought to the prison-house, where she was before, close shut up until the next day. About the time prefixed, the marshall Michaelson came and called hastily for her. When he came into the room, she desired him to stay a little, and speaking mildly to him she said she should be ready presently, even like a sheep prepared for the slaughter. But he in the wolvish nature said he could not wait upon her, but she should now wait upon him. Margaret Smith, her companion, hearing him speak these words with others from the Cain-like spirit, was moved to testify against their unjust laws and proceedings, being grieved to see both him and many others in such gross darkness and hard-heartedness. Then he said, "you shall have your share of the same," with other violent words.

Then they brought her forth, and drums were beat before and behind her, with a band of soldiers, through the town, and so to the place of execution, which is about a mile, the drums being that none might hear her speak all the way.

Some said unto her, that if she would return she might come down and save her life […]. She answered and said, "Nay, I cannot. For in obedience to the will of the Lord God I came, and in his will I abide faithful to the death."

Their Captain, John Webb said, She had been here before, and had the sentence of banishment upon pain of death; and had broken this law in coming again now, as well as formerly; and therefore she was guilty of her own blood. To which M. Dyer said, "Nay, I came to keep blood-guiltiness from you, desiring you to repeal the unrighteous and unjust law of banishment upon pain of death, made against the innocent servants of the Lord. Therefore my blood will be required at your hands, who wilfully do it; but for those that do it in the simplicity of their hearts, I do desire the Lord to forgive them. I came to do the will of my Father, and in obedience to his will I stand even to the death."

John Wilson, their priest of Boston, said, "M. Dyer, O repent; O repent, and be not so deluded and carried away by the deceit of the Devil." M. Dyer answered and said, "Nay, man, I am not now to repent."

Some asked her whether she would have the Elders pray for her. She said, "I know never an Elder here." They asked whether she would have any of the people pray for her. She said she desired the prayers of all the People of God. Some scoffingly said, "It may be she thinks there is none here; this is a mock." M. Dyer looked about and said, "I know but few here."

Then they spake to her again, that one of the Elders might pray for her. She replied and said, "Nay, first a child, then a young woman, then a strong man, before an Elder of Christ Jesus." Some charged her with something that was not understood what it was. But her answer was, "It's false; it's false; I never spoke the words."

Then one said she should say she had been in Paradise. And she answered, "Yea, I have been in Paradise several days." And more she spake of her eternal happiness, that's out of mind. And so sweetly and cheerfully in the Lord she finished her testimony and died a faithful martyr of Jesus Christ.

George Fox in America

George Fox

In August of 1671, the Quaker founder George Fox left England on a visit to the New World. Weakened and infirm after years of persecution and imprisonment, Fox nevertheless made a vigorous tour, visiting Friends in Barbados and Jamaica before doing ministry on the mainland.

American Quakers had already established an excellent relationship with Native Americans, and Fox quickly was drawn to them as well. In the following excerpt, he described a meeting with Indian leaders in Maryland.

Source: George Fox, *The Journal of George Fox*, ed. John L. Nickalls, London: Cambridge University Press, 1952, pp. 617-8.

And it was upon [me] from the Lord to send for the Indian emperor and two of their kings to come to the Firstday's meeting; and the emperor came and stopped all the meeting; but the kings could not reach so far. And when it was done he was very courteous and loving and came and took me by the hand, and I bade Friends take him from the meeting to a Friend's house where I was to lodge that night. And the two kings also came to meet with me and four of their nobles and they stayed all that night and I had two very good speeches to them and they heard the word of the Lord and did confess to it. And what I said to the kings and emperor I desired them to speak to

15

their people, that God is setting up his tabernacle of witnesses in their wilderness countries and setting up his glorious ensign and standard of righteousness. And they asked when we had meetings and they said they would come to them and were very loving. And they said they had a great dispute and a council before they came to me, about their coming.

One Indian leader told Fox of his dislike of the Puritan settlers and their creed—and his all-too-reasonable fear of adopting the Quaker's beliefs.

Source: George Fox, *op. cit.*, p. 624.

In New England there was an Indian king that said he saw that there were many of their people of the Indians turned to the New England professors. He said they were worse since than they were before they left their own religion; and of all religions he said the Quakers were the best. And if they should turn to the New England professors' religion, that made the people worse than they were before, and if he should turn to the Quakers, which was the best, then the professors would hang him and put them to death and banish them as they did the Quakers, and therefore he thought it was the best to be as he was.

Fox's encounters with New England Puritans were contentious and argumentative. In the following excerpt from his journal, he described an episode on Long Island.

Source: George Fox, *op. cit.*, pp. 629-30. (Ellipses indicate a deletion by the editor .)

At Flushing as soon as the meeting was done, there stood up a priest's son and laid down three things that he would dispute, the first was the ordination of ministers, the second women's speaking, and the third that we held a new way of worship. And I spoke to him and demanded what he had against what I had spoken and he could say nothing. Then

I said it was like Christ's way of worship which he set up above 1,600 years ago, and was a new way of worship to him and his priests, it being in the spirit and in the truth. And as for women's speaking, such as the apostles did own I owned, and such as they did deny I did deny.

But what was the priests of New England's ordination? For we do deny them to be as the apostles, for they have not the same spirit as the apostles had, as some of themselves say.

But this priest's son said that their priests had the same spirit as the apostles had.

Then I said to him that they would have the same fruits, and the apostles' spirit did not lead them to cut off people's ears, and to hang and banish them, and imprison, and to spoil people's goods, as they, the priests of New England, had done....

And the priest's son said, for the proof of his priests, that they must go into all nations and preach and give the Supper.

And then I said, "When did any of the priests of New England go into all nations and give them the Supper? For do they go any further than they can have a great or a fat benefice? Or shall people have any Paternoster without the penny?"[1]

Then the priest's son said the priests were of the tribe of Levi.

Then I said that Christ had cut off that tribe of priests of Levi and changed it, and changed and ended the law by which it was made; and Christ came not of the tribe of Levi, but after the order of Mechizideck, and is called the Lion of the tribe of Judah, "And so thou hast cut off all thy priests from being Gospel ministers to be such as deny Christ come in the flesh."[2]

---

[1] Supper refers to Holy Communion; a benefice is a church office; the Paternoster is the Lord's Prayer (Matthew 6:9-13; Luke 11:2-4).

[2] Among the early Israelites, the tribe of Levi produced the priests. Melchizideck (usually spelled Melchizedek or Mechisedek) was a priest and king who blessed Abram (Genesis 14:18-20); the belief that the Christian priesthood comes from his line and not from the Levites is explained in Hebrews 5:6-10; 6:20, 7.

William Penn's "Holy Experiment"

The well-born and well-educated Englishman William Penn was a Quaker by convincement (a term which Friends prefer to "conversion"), and became a tireless advocate for the rights of Friends in Restoration England. A part of him wearied in this task, however. He believed strongly enough in Quaker wisdom to wonder what Friends might accomplish in a world without oppression and persecution. Surely, he believed, they could found a nearly perfect society.

Even while Friends were suffering terrible persecutions in New England, Penn began to consider the possibilities of America. He arbitrated between two Friends concerning the purchase of West New Jersey, then became a partner in the purchase of East New Jersey. But he wanted a territory of his own with which to initiate a "holy experiment."

Charles II owed a large debt to Penn's late father, Admiral Sir William Penn. Instead of money, Penn asked for a large tract of land west of New Jersey. Considering the deal a bargain to himself, Charles complied. The following brief document, dated February 28, 1681 and signed by Solicitor-General Heneage Finch, confirmed Penn's status as Proprietor of a new American colony named after his father.

Source: William Penn, *The Papers of William Penn*, eds. Richard S. Dunn and Mary Maples Dunn, Philadelphia: University of Pennsylvania Press, 1982, Vol. 2, pp. 77-8. (Unusual punctuation, typography, capitalization, and spelling are preserved from the original source.)

His Mat^y is pleased to grant unto William Penn Esqr his Heires and Assignes for ever, a certain Tract of Land in America, to be erected into a province and called by the name of PENSILVANIA. And also to make the said William Penn his Heires and Assignes Cheife Governo^r thereof, With divers p^{r}viledges powers and Authorities granted to the said William penn his Heires and Assignes in Order to the good Governm^t of the said province. Subscribed by Mr Soll^r Grall, by Warrant &t supra.

William Penn, founder and first Proprietor of Philadelphia, meeting the Indians. (Portrayed here by J.L.G. Ferris.)

Penn's Letter to the Lenni Lenape

Like other Quakers before him, William Penn was anxious to establish cordial relations with the Native Americans in his newly-acquired territory. To this end, he made sure not to allow settlement on Indian land which hadn't been fairly purchased from the Indians—despite the fact that, in English eyes, Penn already owned this land. Penn wrote the following letter to the Lenni Lenape (more commonly known as the Delaware Indians) in preparation for making a formal agreement with them.

Source: William Penn, *op. cit.*, pp. 128-9. (Unusual punctuation, typography, capitalization, and spelling are preserved from the original source.)

London: 18th 8mo [October 16]81.

My Freinds

There is one great God and Power that hath made the world and all things therein, to whom you and I and all People owe their being and wellbeing, and to whom you and I must one Day give an account, for all that we do in this world: this great God hath written his law in our hearts, by which we are taught and commanded to love and help and do good

19

to one an other, and not to do harme and mischeif one unto another: Now this great God hath been pleased to make me concerned in yr parts of the World, and the king of the Countrey where I live, hath given unto me a great Province therein, but I desire to enjoy it with your Love and Consent, that we may always live together as Neighbours and freinds, else what would the Great God say to us, who hath made us not to devoure and destroy one an other but live Soberly and kindly together in the world Now I would have you well to observe, that I am very Sensible of the unkindness and Injustice that hath been too much exersised towards you by the People of these Parts off the world, who have sought themselvs, and to make great Advantages by you, rather then be examples of Justice and Goodness unto you, which I hear, hath been matter of trouble to you, and caused great Grudgeings and Animosities, sometimes to the shedding of blood, which hath made the great God Angry. but I am not such a Man, as is well known in my own Country: I have great love and regard towards you, and I desire to Winn and gain your Love & freindship by a kind, just and peaceable life; and the People I send are of the same mind, & shall in all things behave themselves accordingly; and if in any thing any shall offend you or your People, you shall have a full and Speedy Satisfaction for the same by an equall number of honest men on both sides that by no means you may have just Occasion of being offended against them; I shall shortly come to you my selfe. At what time we may more largely and freely confer & discourse of these matters; in the mean time, I have sent my Commissioners to treat with you about land & a firm league of peace. lett me desire you to be kind to them and the People, and receive thes Presents and Tokens which I have sent to you, as a Testimony of my Good will to you, and my resolution to live Justly peaceably and friendly with you, I am your Freind.   Wm Penn

Penn on Pennsylvania's Government

Penn's "holy experiment" in Pennsylvania eventually faltered, and Friends lost political control of the colony. Even so, Penn's political ideas, based on his Quaker idealism, proved an inspiration for future leaders—including those who framed a government for the United States a century later. In 1682, Penn concluded his preface to the First Frame of Government for Pennsylvania with the following passage.

Source: William Penn, *The Witness of William Penn*, ed. Frederick B. Tolles and E. Gordon Alderfer, New York: Macmillan, 1957, pp. 111-2. (Bracketed words are in Tolles and Alderfer's text.)

I know what is said by the several admirers of monarchy, aristocracy, and democracy, which are the rule of one, a few, and many, and are the three common ideas of government, when men discourse of that subject. But I choose to solve the controversy with this small distinction and it belongs to all three: any government is free to the people under it, whatever be the frame, where the laws rule and the people are a party to those laws, and more than this is tyranny, oligarchy, or confusion.

But lastly, when all is said, there is hardly one frame of government in the world so ill-designed by its first founders that in good hands, [it] would not do well enough, and story[3] tells us, the best in ill ones can do nothing that is great or good; witness the Jewish and Roman states. Governments, like clocks, go from the motion men give them, and as governments are made and moved by men, so by them they are ruined too. Wherefore governments rather depend upon men than men upon governments. Let men be good and the government cannot be bad: if it be ill, they will cure it. But if men be bad, let the government be never so good, they will endeavor to warp and spoil it to their turn.

---

[3] History.

I know some say, let us have good laws, and no matter for the men that execute them; but let them consider that though good laws do well, good men do better, for good laws want good men, and be abolished or evaded by ill men, but good men will never want good laws nor suffer ill ones. 'Tis true, good laws have some awe upon ill ministers, but that is where they have not power to escape or abolish them and the people are generally wise and good, but a loose and depraved people (which is the question) love laws and an administration like themselves. That, therefore, which makes a good constitution must keep it; viz., men of wisdom and virtue, qualities that, because they descend not with worldly inheritances, must be carefully propagated by a virtuous education of youth, for which after-ages will owe more to the care and prudence of founders and the successive magistracy than to their parents for their private patrimonies.

These considerations of the weight of government and the nice and various opinions about it made it uneasy to me to think of publishing the ensuing frame and conditional laws, foreseeing both the censures they will meet with from men of differing humors and engagements and the occasion they may give of discourse beyond my design.

But, next to the power of necessity (which is a solicitor that will take no denial) this induced me to a compliance, that we have (with reverence to God and good conscience to men) to the best of our skill contrived and composed the frame and laws of this government to the great end of all government; viz., to support power in reverence with the people and to secure the people from the abuse of power, that they may be free by their just obedience and the magistrates honorable for their just administration; for liberty without obedience is confusion, and obedience without liberty is slavery. To carry this evenness is partly owing to the constitution and partly to the magistracy. Where either of these fail, government will be subject to convulsions, but where both are wanting, it must be totally subverted; then where both meet, the government is like to endure, which I humbly pray and hope God will please to make the lot of this of Pennsylvania. Amen.

WILLIAM PENN

The British made fun of new colonists from England who went to Pennsylvania and bought tracts of land from the Pennsylvania Company (your Quaking Friends). This is one of a deck of illustrated playing cards. (Courtesy of the Bodleian Library, Oxford)

A Philadelphia Meeting

A Quaker Meeting, about 1648, after an engraving by Egbert van Heemskerck

After the founding of Pennsylvania, Friends generally settled into ways similar to those of English Quakers. This was especially true in Penn's model city, Philadelphia, where Quakers conducted silent meetings much as they had in the Old World. In the following segment, Swedish traveler Peter Kalm described a Philadelphia meeting of 1750.

Source: J. William Frost, *The Quaker Family in Colonial America: A Portrait of the Society of Friends,* New York: St. Martin's Press, 1973, pp. 36-7. (Citation by Frost: *Bulletin of Friends' Historical Society*, Philadelphia, 1942, pp. 28-29. Ellipses are in Frost's text.)

Here we sat and waited very quietly from ten o'clock to a quarter after eleven....Finally, one of the two...old men in the front pew rose, removed his hat, turned hither and yon, and began to speak, but so softly that even in the middle of the church, which was not large, it was impossible to hear anything except the confused murmur of the words. Later he began to talk a little louder, but so slowly that four or five minutes elapsed between the sentences; finally the words came bout louder and faster. In their preaching the Quakers have a peculiar mode of expression, which is half singing, with a strange cadence and accent, and ending each cadence, as it were, with a half or...a full sob. Each cadence consists of two, three, or four syllables, but sometimes more, according to the demand of the words and means; e.g. my friends/ /put in your mind/ /we/ /do nothing/ /good of our selves/ /without God's/ /help and assistance/ /etc. In the beginning the sobbing is not heard so plainly, but the deeper and further the speaker gets into his sermon the stronger becomes the sobbing between the cadences. The speaker today made no gestures, but turned in various directions; occasionally he placed one hand on his cheek; and during most of the sermon kept buttoning and unbuttoning his vest with right hand....When he stood for a while using his singsong method he changed his manner of delivery and spoke in a more natural way, or as our ministers do when they say a prayer. Shortly afterwards, however, he began again his half-singing mode of expression, and at the end, just as he was speaking at his best, he stopped abruptly, sat down, and put on his hat.

Conformity of Dress

Also like their Old World counterparts, American Quakers dressed in a manner emphasizing simplicity and conformity. In the following segment, the eighteenth-century Pennsylvanian Jonathan Kirkbride's wardrobe was described by one of his descendents.

Source: Amelia Mott Gummere, *The Quaker: A Study in Costume*, New York: Benjamin Blom, 1901 (reprint, 1968), p. 41. (Citation by Gummere: Mahlon S. Kirkbride, *Domestic Portraiture of our Ancestors Kirkbride; 1650-1824.* Ellipses are in Gummere's text.)

During his preaching expeditions, he went out mounted on a pacing horse, a pair of leather saddle-bags, containing his wardrobe, hung behind the saddle, a silk oil-cloth cover for his hat, and an oilcloth cape over the shoulders, which came down nearly to the saddle, as a protection from storms. Stout corduroy overalls, with rows of buttons down the outside to close them on, protected the breeches and stockings. A light walking stick did double duty, as a cane when on foot, and a riding whip when mounted....

He wore a black beaver hat, with a broad brim turned up at the sides so as to form a point in front and rolled up behind; a drab coat, with broad skirts reaching to the knee, with a low standing collar; a collarless waistcoat, bound at the neck, reaching beyond the hips, with broad pockets, and pocket flaps over them; a white cravat served for a collar; breeches with an opening a few inches above and below the knee, closed with a row of buttons and a silver buckle at the bottom; ample silver buckles to fasten the shoes with; fine yarn stockings....

In winter, shoes gave place to high boots, reaching to the knee in front, and cut lower behind to accommodate the limb.

For a long time, many Quakers considered painted portraits a sinful vanity. They tended not to feel this way about silhouettes.

The Dangers of Nonconformity

Whenever Colonial Quakers deviated from accepted manners of dress or lifestyle, alarm was likely to break out. The following letter of warning was issued by Philadelphia Yearly Meeting in 1726.

Source: Amelia Mott Gummere, *op. cit.*, pp. 152-153. (Unusual punctuation, typography, capitalization, and spelling are preserved from the original source.) [Note: Gummere does not give a citation for this entry.]

From Women ffriends at the yearly Meeting held at Burlington, The 21st. of the 7th Month, 1726.

To Women ffriends at the Several Quarterly & Monthly Meetings belonging to the same,—Greeting.

Dear and Well-beloved Sisters:

A Weighty Concern coming upon many ffaithful ffriends at this Meeting, In Relation to divers undue Liberties that are too frequently taken by some yt. walck among us, & are Accounted of us, We are Willing in the pure Love of Truth wch. hath Mercifully Visited our Souls, Tenderly to Caution & Advise ffriends against those things which we think Inconsistent with our Ancient Christian Testimony of Plainness in Apparel &c., Some of which we think it proper to Particularize.

As first, That Immodest ffashion of hooped Pettycoats, or ye. imitation of them, Either by Something put into their Pettycoats to make ym sett full, or Wearing more than is Necessary, or any other Imitation Whatsoever, Which we take to be but a Branch Springing from ye. same Corrupt root of Pride.

And also That None of Sd ffriends Accustom themselves to wear their Gowns with Superfluous ffolds behind, but plain and Decent. Nor to go without Aprons, Nor to wear Superfluous Gathers or Pleats in their Capps or Pinners, Nor to wear their heads drest high behind, Neither to Cut or Lay their hair on ye fforehead or Temples.

And that ffriends are careful to avoid Wearing of Stript Shoos, or Red or White heel'd Shoos, or Clogs, or Shoos trimmed wh. Gawdy Colours.

Likewise, That all ffriends be Careful to Avoid Superfluity of Furniture in their Houses, And as much as may be to refrain Using Gawdy floured or Stript Callicos and Stuffs.

And also that no ffriends Use ye Irreverent practice of taking Snuff, or handing Snuff boxes one to Another in Meetings.

Also that ffriends Avoid ye Unnecessary use of ffans in Meetings, least it Divert ye mind from ye more Inward & Spiritual Exercise wch. all ought to be Concern'd in.

And also That ffriends do not Accustom themselves to go in bare Breasts or bare Necks.

There is Likewise a Tender Concern upon o^r minds to recommend unto all ffriends, the Constant use of ye plain Language It being a Branch of our Ancient Christian Testimony, for wch. many of or Worthy Elders underwent deep Sufferings in their Day As they Likewise Did because they could not give ye Common Salutation by Bowing and Cringing of ye Body wch. we Earnestly desire ffriends may be Careful to Avoid.

And we farther Tenderly Advise and Exhort That all ffriends be careful to Maintain Love and Unity and to Watch against Whisperings and Evil Surmisings One against Another, and to keep in Humility, That Nothing be done through Strife or Vainglory, and yt. those who are Concerned to take an oversight over the fflock, Do it not as Lords over God's heritage, but as Servants to ye Churches.

Dear Sisters, These Things we Solidly recommend to yor Care and Notice In a Degree of yt. Divine Love wch hath previously Manifested Itself for ye Redemption of a [MS. illegible] ye Vain Conversations, Customs, & Fashions yt. are in ye World, That we might be unto ye Lord, a Chosen Generation, A Royal Priesthood, An Holy Nation, A Peculair People, Shewing forth ye Praises of him who hath called us out of Darkness into his Marvellous Light, that We may all walck as Children of the Light & of ye Day, Is ye Earnest Desire of our Souls.

We Conclude wth. ye Salutation of Unfeigned Love, yor ffriends and Sisters.

Signed on behalf & by ord^r. of ye s^d. Meeting By
HANNAH HILL.

Ann Cooper Whitall's Journal

Even in hospitable territories like New Jersey and Pennsylvania, life for Quaker colonists was often hard—perhaps especially for the women, who endured the brunt of domestic tragedies. For example, Ann Cooper Whitall was a simple, semi-literate woman who lived only about a day's journey from the great city of Philadelphia, but still suffered all the dangers and deprivations of the frontier. She constantly worried about cruel weather, the illnesses of her children, and Indian attacks. By Whitall's time, the goodwill between whites and Native Americans had waned, partly because of the policies of William Penn's less-idealistic son Thomas. Whitall was also discouraged that her husband was so often away from home.

The following excerpt from her journal, written in 1760, describes an oasis of faith and hope in Whitall's bitter and difficult life—the comfort and preachings of two Quaker women ministers.

Source: Elisabeth Potts Brown and Susan Mosher Stuard, eds., *Witnesses for Change: Quaker Women over Three Centuries*, New Brunswick: Rutgers University Press, pp. 87-8. (Citation in *Witnesses for Change*: The Quaker Collection at Haverford College; bracketed portions are in *Witnesses for Change*.)

10th day of the 4th Month, our dear friend Mary Kirby was here at Woodbury and Elizabeth Smith from Burlington, New Jersey, and she spoke first, and spoke as if some was likely for [to] miss their way by not giving heed to the Inward Guide. Oh, what a sad case is this; then Mary told us of sleeping in Meeting. She felt it among us, some would dress like others and go like them to Meeting but that would not do for they would be like the Foolish Virgins [who] had no oil in their lamps.[4] She told us of them over and over again with a great deal of sorrow. What did we do for ourselves she said, when we were asleep? Oh, this part that never dies. I rejoiced to hear her tell us of sleeping in Meeting!

---

[4] See Matthew 25:1-12.

Being in great hopes it might do some good. Desiring I might be favored with a sense of my own condition and see my own failings. And she told us of the warnings we have had many times from sometimes [ago when] we were in a little. Oh, or dread when one did die out of the house. We could think then that we must go hence. But that would be all forgot. We live in plenty, she said, we did not want bread. Oh, what a hard thing would that be, we did not know, no, how soon that would be. Oh, that we might be thankful receivers of all these wonderful favors and blessings we have of the Mighty One. She said there was many a cold home and she did believe there would be more cold homes. Oh, prepare, prepare for this change. We know it must come and we know not how soon and how can we be so dead?

She got up again and spoke so to the afflicted ones [that they] be so afflicted every way that [they] knew not what to do nor which way to turn but it was often her lot to be so overwhelmed in sorrow and in grief. Well, she said, the world loved its own but not the sorrowful and mourners; well, in this sorrowful condition she said was the time to say Glory, Glory to his Mighty Name that brings sorrow. Oh come death, come life, come what will, come, we will serve the Above. All, oh glory, glory to His Mighty Name. She said, oh, these mourners that have no comfort in nothing that they think is not a serving of their Mighty Maker.

Matters of Conscience

Ever since Friends arrived in the New World, they have had a remarkable impact on American public issues. This may seem surprising, since Quakerism, with its emphasis on the Inward Light, is a uniquely intimate and private faith. Indeed, many of its followers have struggled to stay as much as possible out of the public, political sphere. But from the beginning, events in Quaker history have conspired to make this difficult. Their early persecution in England, for example, compelled Friends to petition political leaders and even the King for justice. It was largely because of Quaker efforts that Parliament passed the Toleration Act of 1689.

The situation in the United States has been similar. American Friends have struggled with the question of whether to pursue their lives in simple purity and let the world go its way, or to carry their faith into the world and try to improve the lot of all humanity. Many Friends have made the latter choice, involving themselves in such issues as prison reform, care of the mentally ill, Native American rights, and relief for the poor. This chapter offers a small sampling of American Quaker activities in three issues of public life: abolition of slavery, women's rights, and pacifism.

Friends on Slavery

Because of their belief that every human being contained a spark of God, Quakers could hardly justify the enslavement of millions of people in the New World. And indeed, by the time Abraham Lincoln was born in 1809, no Quakers owned slaves. But after that time, their actions in the cause of abolitionism varied. Some Friends believed it morally sufficient to have rid themselves of the taint of slavery. Others considered it important to actively pursue the end of slavery. The following segments are by three Quaker abolitionists.

The Abolitionism of John Woolman

Surely no Quaker of the Eighteenth Century did more for the cause of abolitionism than John Woolman. It was largely because of his efforts that the Friends rid themselves of slaves. Woolman's commitment to abolition was so complete that he refused even to use slave-produced products, including clothing dye. This made his already-austere Quaker wardrobe appear quite startling.

Woolman's efforts against slavery were partly motivated by something which happened to him when he was a young shop assistant. He described this incident in the following passage from his famous Journal. *It was an instance, he felt, of his own failure to act on principle. He rarely if ever failed in such a way again.*

Source: John Woolman, *The Journal and Other Writings*, intro. Vida D. Scudder, London: J. M. Dent, 1910, pp. 26-7.

My Employer having a Negro Woman, sold her, and desired me to write a Bill of Sale, the Man being waiting who bought her: The Thing was sudden; and, though the Thoughts of writing an Instrument of Slavery for one of my Fellow-creatures felt uneasy, yet I remembered I was hired by the Year, that it was my Master who directed me to do it, and that it was an elderly Man, a Member of our Society, who bought her; so, through Weakness, I gave way, and wrote; but, at the executing it, I was so afflicted in my Mind, that I said, before my Master and the Friend, that I believed Slave-keeping to be a Practice inconsistent with the *Christian* Religion: This in some Degree abated my Uneasiness; yet, as often as I reflected seriously upon it, I thought I should have been clearer, if I had desired to have been excused from it, as a Thing against my Conscience; for such it was. And, some Time after this, a young Man, of our Society, spoke to me to write a Conveyance of a Slave to him, he having lately taken a Negro into his House: I told him I was not easy to write it; for, though many of our Meeting and in other Places kept Slaves, I still believed the Practice was not right, and desired to be excused from the writing. I spoke to him in Good-will; and he told me that keeping Slaves was not altogether agreeable to his Mind; but that the Slave being a Gift to his Wife, he had accepted of her.

Throughout his life, Woolman traveled a great deal in both America and Britain, testifying against slavery and the slave trade wherever he went. In this typical passage from his Journal, *Woolman described his debates with two men about slavery.*

Source: John Woolman, *op. cit.*, pp. 53-5.

…[O]n the Way we happening in Company with a Colonel of the Militia, who appeared to be a thoughtful Man, I took Occasion to remark on the Difference in general betwixt a People used to labour moderately for their Living, training up their Children in Frugality and Business, and those who live on the Labour of Slaves; the former, in my View, being the most happy Life: With which he concurred, and mentioned the Trouble arising from the untoward, slothful, Disposition of the Negroes; adding, that one of our Labourers would do as much in a Day as two of their Slaves. I replied, that free Men, whose Minds were properly on their Business, found a Satisfaction in improving, cultivating, and providing for their Families; but Negroes, labouring to support others who claim them as their Property, and expecting nothing but Slavery during Life, had not the like Inducement to be industrious.

After some farther Conversation, I said, that Men having Power too often misapplied it; that though we made Slaves of the Negroes, and the *Turks* made Slaves of the *Christians*, I believed that Liberty was the natural Right of all Men equally: Which he did not deny; but said, the Lives of the Negroes were so wretched in their own Country, that many of them lived better here than there: I only said, there are great odds, in regard to us, on what Principle we act; and so the Conversation on that Subject ended: And I may here add, that another Person, some Time Afterward, mentioned the Wretchedness of the Negroes, occasioned by their intestine Wars, as an Argument in Favour of our fetching them away for Slaves: To which I then replied, if Compassion on the *Africans*, in Regard to their domestic Troubles, were the real Motive of our purchasing them, that Spirit of Tenderness, being attended to, would incite us to use them kindly, that, as Strangers brought out of Affliction, their Lives might be happy among us; and as they are human Creatures, whose Souls are as precious as ours, and who may receive the same Help and Comfort from the holy Scriptures as we do, we could not omit suitable Endeavours to instruct them therein: But while we manifest, by our conduct, that our Views in purchasing them are to advance ourselves; and while our buying Captives taken in War animates those Parties to push on that War, and increase Desolation amongst them, to say they live unhappy in *Africa*, is far from being an Argument in our Favour: And I farther said, the present Circumstances of these Provinces to me appear difficult; that the Slaves look like a burthensome Stone to such who burthen themselves with them; and that if the white People retain a Resolution to prefer their outward Prospects of Gain to all other Considerations, and do not act conscientiously toward them as fellow Creatures, I believe that Burthen will grow heavier and heavier, till Times change in a Way disagreeable to us: At which the Person appeared very serious, and owned, that, in considering their Condition, and the Manner of their Treatment in these Provinces, he had sometimes thought it might be just in the Almighty so to order it.

Lucretia Mott on Slavery

Lucretia Mott

Quaker Lucretia Mott was a nineteenth-century activist concerned with such matters as poverty, pacifism, temperance, Native American rights, capital punishment, and feminism. She addressed the issue of abolitionism in the following excerpt from an 1841 Boston sermon.

Source: Lucretia Mott, *Lucretia Mott: Her Complete Speeches and Sermons*, ed. Dana Greene, New York: Edwin Mellen Press, 1980, pp. 31-2.

The time will not permit me to enlarge, or I would turn your attention to further applications of gospel principles, and remind you, as we examined them together, that "he that doeth righteous is righteous," of whatever sect or clime.

I am aware that, in this city, the appeal has often been made to you in behalf of the suffering slave. I am sensible that most able appeals have been frequent here; but the time has come for you, not merely to listen to them, but to seek for the means of aiding in the working of this righteousness. Whether you should act in organized societies, or as individuals, it is not for me to decide for any; but we all have a part of the work to perform, for we are all implicated in the transgression. Let us examine our own clothing—the furniture of our houses—the conducting of trade—the affairs of commerce—and then ask ourselves, whether we have not each, as individuals, a duty which, in some way or other, we are bound to perform.

When I look only over professing Christendom my soul mourns over the doom to perpetual and unrequitted toil, the entire deprivation of rights, the outrage of human affections, and the absence of all that makes life desirable, which all unite to weigh down the lives of so many millions, while so few are ready to raise the cry of justice and mercy on their behalf. Are there not men and women here, whom these things shall yet constrain to exertion, that they may be remedied? In how many ways may you not exercise your various powers for the alleviation of the miseries of those whose sufferings we have contemplated! You have pens and voices to commend their cause to others, and to portray their miseries so as to gain sympathy. To how many towns you might go, and awaken their inhabitants to the relief of these sufferings!

Levi Coffin and the Underground Railroad

Levi Coffin (Courtesy of the Levi Coffin House)

While many Friends like Lucretia Mott sought to end slavery through legal means, others took more drastic action. Some Friends participated in the Underground Railroad. This was a widespread, organized effort (led primarily by free African-Americans) to help escaped slaves make their ways to freedom. It has been estimated that between 50,000 and 100,000 slaves were assisted by this effort.

Quaker Levi Coffin became known as the "President of the Underground Railroad." He and his wife Catherine are believed to have assisted over 3,000 slaves. On one occasion in Cincinnati, Ohio, Coffin found it necessary to buy a carriage to transport an escaped slave couple to Canada. Coffin openly solicited funds from local businessmen. With characteristic Quaker directness, he solicited their compassion as well.

Source: Levi Coffin, *Reminiscences of Levi Coffin, the Reputed President of the Underground Railroad*, ed. Ben Richmond, Richmond, Indiana: Friends United Press, 1991, pp. 214-6.

...I next called at a wholesale grocery on Pearl Street, where I had business to transact. I knew that the principal member of the firm was not in sympathy with my anti-slavery work, but resolved to speak to him on the matter. Meeting him at the door, I introduced the subject, and the following conversation took place:

"Hast thou any stock in the Underground Railroad, Friend?"

"No!"

"It pays well; thou ought to take stock; it makes one feel good every time he is called on for an assessment."

"I want nothing to do with it. I don't believe in helping fugitives."

"Stop, my good friend, I don't believe thou knowest what thou art talking about. Suppose thy wife had been captured and carried off by Indians or Algerines, had suffered all the cruelties and hardships of slavery, and had escaped barefooted, bareheaded and with but little clothing, and must perish without aid, or be recaptured and taken back into slavery; suppose some one was to interest himself in her behalf and call on me to aid in restoring her to freedom, and I should refuse to do it and say, 'I want nothing to do with helping fugitives'—what wouldst thou think of me?"

"I do not expect my wife ever to be in such a condition."

"I hope she will not be, but I know of somebody's wife who is in just such a condition now, and I have been called on for help. It always does me good to have the opportunity to help in such cases, and as I am never permitted to enjoy any good thing without wishing others to partake with me, I thought I would give thee the opportunity to enjoy this with me." Then I told him of the man and wife who were sold to a negro-trader to be taken to the far South, and related how they made their escape, bareheaded, barefooted and thinly clad, and hastened to the Ohio River in the dark, over ten miles or more of rough road, while their hearts were full of fear and dread lest they should be recaptured. At the river they found a skiff which they succeeded in breaking loose, and crossed safely to the city, where they found good quarters. I said: "Great exertions have been made to find them and drag them back to slavery, but the efforts have not succeeded;

the fugitives have been kept in close quarters. We think now that it may be safe to forward them on the Underground Railroad to Canada, but they must be suitably provided for the journey, and money must be raised to help them on their way. Now I want thee to take stock and help us clothe and forward these people; I know thou wouldst feel better to contribute for their relief. Now I have done my duty; I have given thee the opportunity to contribute, and if thou art not disposed to do so, it is thy look-out, not mine." I then left him and went into the counting-room to transact some business with the bookkeeper. When this was done, I turned to go, but as I was passing out of the store the merchant, who was waiting on a customer, called to me. I stopped, and he came to me and said in a low tone;

"I will give you a trifle if you want something."

I replied: "I want nothing; but if it is thy desire to contribute something to help those poor fugitives I told thee about, I will see that it is rightly applied."

The merchant then handed me a silver half-dollar. I took it, and said: "Now I know thou wilt feel better," then left the store. About a week afterward I was passing down Walnut Street, below Fourth, when I saw this merchant coming up on the opposite side. When he saw me, he crossed over and coming up to me, smiling, he shook hands and asked in a whisper: "Did they get off safely?"

I laughed outright and exclaimed "Ah, thou hast taken stock in the Underground Railroad, and feels an interest in it; if thou hadst not taken stock thou wouldst have cared nothing about it. Yes, they got off safely and by this time are probably in Canada."

Quaker Feminists

Early Quaker leaders like George Fox and Margaret Fell assumed that women contained a spark of divinity as surely as did men. Following in this belief, many Quaker women (including Alice Paul, the author of the Equal Rights Amendment) have been active and influential feminists. The following segments offer samples of the thinking of two nineteenth-century Quaker feminists.

Lucretia Mott

In 1840, the Quaker abolitionist Lucretia Mott went to an international anti-slavery conference in London, only to learn that she could not serve as a delegate—largely because she was a woman. Mott was already a feminist, but this incident increased her fervor for the cause of women's rights. Her life-long dedication became an inspiration to younger feminists, including Elizabeth Cady Stanton. When the Equal Rights Amendment was first proposed in 1923, it was called the "Lucretia Mott Amendment."

Mott considered it essential that women be as free to follow the dictates of the Inward Light as were men. But how was this possible if women were denied opportunities to contribute to reform, as she herself had been in London? She discussed this question in the following excerpt from an 1849 sermon delivered in Philadelphia.

Source: Lucretia Mott, *op. cit.*, pp. 147-8.

This age is notable for its works of mercy and benevolence—for the efforts that are made to reform the inebriate and the degraded, to relieve the oppressed and the suffering. Women as well as men are interested in these works of justice and mercy. They are efficient co-workers, their talents are called into profile exercise, their labors are effective in each department of reform. The blessing to the merciful, to the peacemaker is equal to man and to woman. It is greatly to be deplored, now that she is increasingly qualified for usefulness, that any view should be presented, calculated to retard her labors of love.

Why should not woman seek to be a reformer? If she is to shrink from being such an iconoclast as shall "break the image of man's lower worship," as so long held up to view; if she is to fear to exercise her reason, and her noblest powers, lest these should be thought to "attempt to act the man," and not "acknowledge his supremacy"; if she is to be satisfied with the narrow sphere assigned her by man, nor aspire to a higher, lest she should transcend the bounds of female delicacy; truly it is a mournful prospect for woman. We would admit all the difference, that our great and beneficent Creator has made, in the relation of man and woman, nor would we seek to disturb this relation; but we deny that the present position of woman is her true sphere of usefulness; nor will she attain to this sphere, until the disabilities and disadvantages, religious, civil, and social, which impede her progress, are removed out of her way. These have enervated her mind and paralysed her powers. While man assumes that the present is the original state designed for woman, that the *existing* "differences are not arbitrary nor the result of accident," but grounded in nature; she will not make the necessary effort to obtain her just rights, lest it should subject her to the kind of scorn and contemptuous manner in which she has been spoken of.

So far from her "ambition leading her to attempt to act the man," she needs all the encouragement she can receive, by the removal of obstacles from her path, in order that she may become a "true woman." As it is desirable that man should act a manly and generous part, not "mannish," so let woman be urged to exercise a dignified and womanly bearing, not womanish. Let her cultivate all the graces and proper accomplishments of her sex, but let not these degenerate into a kind of effeminacy, in which she is satisfied to be the mere plaything or toy of society, content with her outward adorning, and with the tone of flattery and fulsome adulation too often addressed to her. True, nature has made a difference in her configuration, her physical strength, her voice, &c.— and we ask no change, we are satisfied with nature. But how has neglect and mismanagement increased this difference! It is our duty to develop these natural powers by suitable exercise, so that they may be strengthened "by reason of use." In the ruder state of society, woman is made to bear heavy burdens, while her "lord and master" walks idly by her side. In the civilization to which we have attained, if cultivated and refined woman could bring all her powers into use, she might engage in pursuits which she now shrinks from as beneath her proper vocation. The energies of men need not then be wholly devoted to the counting house and common business of life, in order that women in fashionable society may be supported in their daily promenades and nightly visits to the theatre and ball room.

Susan B. Anthony

Also a Quaker, Susan B. Anthony was inspired by the work of the older Lucretia Mott. Like Mott, she devoted herself to many issues of reform, including abolition and temperance. She never lived to see the achievement of her prized goal, the right of American women to vote. But when, fourteen years after her death, the Nineteenth Amendment to the Constitution gave women that right, it was known as the "Anthony Amendment."

At a meeting of progressive Friends in 1857, Anthony confronted spiritualist-reformer Andrew Jackson Davis concerning his outdated concepts of womanhood, stirring a long and vigorous debate concerning the nature of the sexes. She described this debate in the following excerpt from a letter to her friend and fellow-feminist Elizabeth Cady Stanton.

Source: Elizabeth Cady Stanton and Susan B. Anthony, *The Elizabeth Cady Stanton-Susan B. Anthony Reader*, revised edition, ed. Ellen Carol DuBois, Boston: Northeastern University Press, 1992, pp. 65-7. (Citation by DuBois: Library of Congress, Stanton Papers. Bracketed portions and ellipses are in DuBois's text.)

Susan B. Anthony

Mrs. D. from the Committee read a paper on Womans Rights going back to Woman's position in marriage as the starting point. *Mr.* Davis spoke first. He set forth his idea of the nature of the sexes and their relation to each [other]. Spoke truthfully and nobly of re-production, of the *abuses* in marriage etc, etc. But to his idea of the sexes, he said woman's inherent nature *is Love and Man's Wisdom.* That Love reaches out to Wisdom, Man, and Wisdom reaches out to Love, Woman, and the two meet and make a beautiful blending of the two principles....

My soul was on fire. This is but a *revamp* of the world's idea from the beginning, the very same doctrine that consigned woman from the beginning to the sphere of all affections, that subjugated her to man's wisdom....The question was *called for.* I *must out,* and said Mr. President, I must say a word, and I did say a word. I said *Women.* If you accept the theory given you by Davis, you may give up all talk of a change for woman: she is now where God and nature intended she should be. If it be a fact that the principle of Wisdom is indigenous in Man, and Love an exotic, then must wisdom *prevail,* and so with woman, must *Love prevail.*

Therefore woman must look to *man* for *Wisdom,* must ever feel it impossible for her to attain Wisdom equal to him. Such a doctrine makes my heart *sink* within me, said I. And did I accept it, I would return to my own Father's house, and never again raise my voice for woman's right to the control of her own person, the ownership of her own earnings, the guardianship of her own children. For if this be true, she ought not to possess those rights. She ought to make final appeal to the wisdom of her husband, father and brother. My word stirred the waters, and brought Davis to his feet again, but he failed to extricate himself from the conclusions to which his premises philosophically lead. Well Sunday, there were more than a *thousand* people congregated, hundreds more *out* than in doors....

All day yesterday, the likeness and unlikeness of the sexes has been the topic of discussion. Phillip D. Moore of Newark N.J. took sides with me. Says my note at Waterloo, last spring, was the *first* he ever heard sounded on that side, and there he came forthwith to me and expressed his sympathy. Well on the Love and Wisdom side, we had [Aaron M.] Powell, George Taylor, Dr. Mary Taylor of Buffalo, and a Mr. Lloyd of Pa. The discussion has been loud and long, and how I wished that *you* could be here. I tell you, Mrs. Stanton, after all, it is very *precious* to the soul of man, that he shall *reign supreme in intellect*, and it will take Centuries if not ages to dispossess him of the fancy that he is born to do so.

Mr. Moore and the Listeners, two women and one man, sound, sensible people, say I sustained my position by *fact* and argument. The Female Doctor urged as a Physiological fact that *girl babies* have from their births less physical vigor, than the boy baby. Then she claimed that there is ever passing from the Woman out to Man a "female arrow," influence she meant, that thrills his soul, all unlike that of man to man etc. Well then here is a fact, a girl dressed in boy's clothes stands at a type case side by side with a young man for three years, and this "female arrow" is never perceived, at least

45

not sufficiently to cause the recipient to suspect the sex at his side [is] other than his own.

Take that same being, array her in woman's dress, and tomorrow morning place her at the same case. While the tones of her voice, the move of her hand, the glance of her eye are all the same as yesterday, her presence causes the sensuous thrill to rush to his very fingers and toes ends. Now tell me the cause. Is the "arrow" in the being, does it go out to that young man from the brain, the soul, the femininity of that young woman, or is it the flowing robes and waving tresses, in the *knowledge* of the *difference* of *sex*. *The latter I say*. At least to a very great extent. But, say our opponents, such an admission is so gross, so animal. Well I can't help that. *If it is fact*, there it is. To me it is not coarse or gross, it is simply the answering of the highest and holiest function of the physical organism, that is that of *reproduction*. To be a *Mother*, to be a *Father* is the last and highest wish of any human being, to *re-produce himself* or *herself*. The accomplish [ment] of this purpose is only through the meeting of the sexes. And when we come into the presence of one of the opposite sex, who embodies what to us seems the true and the noble and the beautiful, our souls are stirred, and whether we realize it or not, it is a thrill of joy that such qualities are reproducible *and* that we may be the *agents*, the *artists* in such re-production. It is the *knowledge* that the two together may be the instruments, that shall execute a work so *God like*.

Friends in Times of War

As with many other tenets of Quakerism, George Fox set the original precedent for pacifism. Very early in his ministry, he refused a captaincy in Cromwell's army: "...I told them I lived in the virtue of that life and power that took away the occasion of all wars" (George Fox, The Journal of George Fox, *ed. John L. Nickalls, London: Cambridge University Press, 1952, p. 65)* *...This became known as the Quaker "Peace Testimony." It was made official by Fox's disciple (and eventually his wife) Margaret Fell in 1660, when she included it in a document addressed to the King and Parliament.*

Friends have been reluctant to take up arms ever since. While many Quakers have considered pacifism a personal, private matter, others have gone into the political arena to oppose and protest warfare in any form. Quaker pacifism has often led to difficulties and moral dilemmas, as the following segments suggest.

Quaker Pacifism During the American Revolution

During the Revolutionary War, the loyalties of Colonial Friends were torn between British rule and the American cause. But few Friends believed that independence from Britain, whatever its advantages, was worth the price of war. Accordingly, Quakers generally refused to fight or to support independence. Those who broke with this policy were often disowned by the Society of Friends. The following is an excerpt from a tract published by a Quaker meeting in Philadelphia on January 20, 1776.

Source: William Dudley, ed., *The American Revolution: Opposing Viewpoints®*, San Diego: Greenhaven Press, 1992, pp. 165-6. (Citation by Dudley: *The Ancient Testimony and Principles of the People Called Quakers, Renewed with Respect to the King and Government; and Touching the Commotions now prevailing in these and other Parts of America*, 1776.)

When we consider—That at the time they [the colonists' ancestors] were persecuted and subject to severe sufferings, as a people unworthy of the benefits of religious or civil society, the hearts of the king and rulers, under whom they thus suffered, were inclined to grant them these fruitful countries, and entrust them with charters of very extensive powers and privileges.—That on their arrival here, the minds of the natives were inclined to receive them with great hospitality and friendship, and to cede to them the most valuable part of their land on very easy terms.—That while the principles of justice and mercy continued to preside, they were preserved in tranquility and peace, free from the desolating calamities of war; and their endeavours were wonderfully blessed and prospered; so that the saying of the wisest of kings was signally verified to them, "When a man's ways please the Lord, he maketh even his enemies to be at peace with him." Prov. xvi. 7.

The benefits, advantages, and favour, we have experienced by our dependence on, and connection with, the kings and government, under which we have enjoyed this happy state, appear to demand from us the greatest circumspection, care and constant endeavours, to guard against every attempt to alter, or subvert, that dependence and connection.

The scenes lately presented to our view, and the prospect before us, we are sensible, are very distressing and discouraging. And though we lament that such amicable measures, as have been proposed, both here and in England, for the adjustment of the unhappy contests subsisting, have not yet been effectual; nevertheless, we should rejoice to observe the continuance of mutual peaceable endeavours for effecting a reconciliation; having grounds to hope that the divine favour and blessing will attend them.

It hath ever been our judgment and principle, since we were called to profess the Light of Christ Jesus, manifested in our consciences, unto this day, that the setting up, and putting down kings and governments, is God's peculiar prerogative; for causes best known to himself: and that it is not our business to have any hand or contrivance therein: nor to be busy-bodies above our station, much less to plot and contrive the ruin, or overturn any of them; but to pray for the king, and safety of our nation, and good of all men; that we may live a peaceable and quiet life, in all godliness and honesty, under the government which God is pleased to set over us. Ancient Testimony, 1696, in Sewell's History.[5]

May we therefore firmly unite in the abhorrence of all such writings and measures, as evidence a desire and design to break off the happy connection we have heretofore enjoyed with the kingdom of Great Britain, and our just and necessary subordination to the king, and those who are lawfully placed in authority under him; that thus the repeated solemn declarations made on this subject, in the addresses sent to the king on behalf of the people of America in general, may be confirmed, and remain to be our firm and sincere intentions to observe and fulfil.

Emily Greene Balch: The Challenge of World War II

The Quaker Peace Testimony faced a particular challenge at the outset of World War II. Could Friends wholeheartedly declare nonresistance to an enemy like Hitler, who invaded nations, despised democracy, espoused genocidal racism, and spoke of world domination?

The largely Quaker-led Women's International League for Peace and Freedom struggled with this question. While United States members agreed to promote American neutrality, they were divided between two different kinds of neutrality. Mandatory neutrality made no distinction between aggressor and victims. Discretionary neutrality sought to penalize aggressors and to aid victims. To absolute pacifists, discretionary neutrality seemed perilously close to participating in the war. Most American members of the WILPF supported mandatory neutrality, much to the frustration of European members.

---

[5] Willem Sewel was an early Quaker historian.

WILPF leader Emily Greene Balch, a convinced Quaker, had lost her professorship at Wellesley College because of her opposition to American involvement in World War I. She was by no means so certain of her pacifistic stand shortly before America's entry into World War II, as she indicated in these excerpts from a private letter to Alice Hamilton, written in 1941. She ultimately favored discretionary neutrality.

Source: Elisabeth Potts Brown and Susan Mosher Stuard, eds., *Witnesses for Change: Quaker Women over Three Centuries*, New Brunswick: Rutgers University Press, pp. 153-5. (Citation in *Witnesses for Change*: Emily Green Balch to Alice Hamilton, 20 February 1941, in the WILDPF Papers-U.S. Section, Records, DG 43, Series C., Box 37, SCBC. Ellipses indicate deletions by the editor of this volume.)

People say this country is confused, divided and chaotic, etc. I must say that it appears to me that the great mass are united to a surprising degree and with no more than quite wholesome divergences. I seem to see: wide agreement *on aid of all kinds to Britain short of war*; somewhat smaller body of opinion within this ready successively for a) policy that risks war, b) military intervention (much smaller). Then, on the other end: a) opposition due to fear of excessive executive power, b) pagan isolationism which, in my opinion, has no leg to stand on, either realist or moral, c) those who believe one should begin with making democracy (nearly) perfect in the U.S. and *then* concern ourselves with helping to clean up other peoples' messes. ("Charity begins at home" to [sic] often means "and ends there.")

It is *not* enough to sweep before your own door, nor to cultivate your own garden, nor to put out the fire when your own house is burning and "disinterest yourself," as the diplomats say, when the frame house next door is in flames and the children calling from its nursery windows to be taken out.

d) Then there are the 100% absolutist religious pacifists— of whom I have never been one.

I stop being non-resistant when it is a question of offering my neighbor's cheek for the blow. As a matter of fact I am not 100% non-resistant even in what concerns only myself.

At the same time I thank God for the Conscientious Objectors. There are not enough of them to prevent action and they are highly educational and their purity, if not true wisdom, is a definite contribution to present and future. They fulfill the function which Elwood Trueblood in his excellent article in the December *Atlantic* accepts as the sole justification for pacifism—that of "bearing witness." I am glad some have the vocation for this, though I have not....

I am far from admitting that it is not true as we Quakers believe, that "there is that of God in everyman." But I do not believe that there is *now* "that" in Hitler et al. that responds with magnanimity to the non-resistant virtues. I would not say they "understand nothing but force," but I would say that they make a religion of force which makes them impervious along those lines. At the same time they may be capable of more "sacrificial" self-giving than we are to what they believe is the cause of advance. Alas, this seems to mean to them "Woe to the weak." "Liquidate the 'other'"—(Jew Pole Negro). "Make straight the path for the powerful, able, noble master-race. This is the way of the Gods."

I believe this is devil's doctrine but not that the men who are hypnotized by it are necessarily devils....

I am not at all sure Willkie[6] is not right in believing that *as things are now* our best chance of peace as a nation (to say nothing of world peace) is to help to try to put down Hitlerism.

I am not very hopeful. I *am* afraid. I cannot feel that there is now any path that has a chance of leading forward that is not a bloody one and a long one.

My position is that peoples by their crimes and blunders can get themselves into a position where on the *plane of political action* there is only a choice of evils.

One can withdraw from this world and let it go on its

---

[6] Wendell Willkie, American politician, was the Republican presidential nominee in 1940. He lost to Franklin D. Roosevelt.

own wicked way. If one feels it is a duty to *stay in the world* and try to make it better in such ways as are practically open to one, then one is in for all the intolerable consequences of the fighting method and its competition in the cruelist [sic] of "skin games"[7] (referring to Galsworthy's wonderful play of that name). And perhaps hunger blockade is the most disastrous weapon of all.

Edwin Bronner on the Vietnam Moratorium

Many American Friends did not feel the same moral uncertainties about the war in Vietnam they had felt concerning World War II. To them, the United States had no part in a conflict so far away, in which American interests were so peripheral. Accordingly, many Quakers took part in protests against the war, and the American Friends Service Committee (founded by Friends in 1917 to carry out humanitarian efforts) offered aid and relief to victims and casualties on both sides of the conflict.

In 1969, while the Nixon administration was claiming the support of a "Great Silent Majority" for continued involvement in the war, the Vietnam Moratorium March on Washington took place. Many Friends were there, including historian Edwin Bronner, who expressed the following thoughts about this event.

Source: Daisy Newman, *A Procession of Friends: Quakers in America*, New York: Doubleday, 1972, p. 419. (Citation by Newman: *Friends Journal*, December 15, 1969. Ellipses are in Newman's text.)

While walking up Pennsylvania Avenue Saturday afternoon, surrounded by thousands of my fellow Americans bent on influencing our government to change its policy, my thoughts went to other persons and groups that have traveled on that historic highway…my mind centered on those who, though in the minority, turned out to be right, while the majority was wrong. I thought of Abraham Lincoln, who went up and down that avenue, the last time in a coffin. I remembered

[7] "Skin game" means swindling trick.

that he voted against the Mexican War[8] forty-seven times. …There were…the valiant souls who demanded equal rights for women.…Quaker women, and many others…marched on Pennsylvania Avenue in 1913 and the fact that a "silent majority" opposed their campaign did not dissuade them.…

There was unpleasantness around us on Pennsylvania Avenue some of the time. Most of us were quiet, peaceful, and cooperative. Some were noisy, militant, abrasive. I remember that not all persons who have been right in our history were respectable, cooperative, and lovable. Benjamin Lay, the dwarf who needled Quakers…came to mind—Benjamin Lay, who sprinkled Friends with pig's blood, to remind them of the blood of slaves…[9]

Finally, my mind moved to a recent novel, Jessamyn West's Except for Me and Thee…the saga of the Birdwells, patterned on her Milhous ancestors.…[10] These Quaker ancestors of Jessamyn West heard the clear call to a higher law than the Fugitive Slave Law of 1850,[11] and obeyed the still small voice within them.

Those of us who cry out against the war in Vietnam, who demonstrate in Washington…may not be in the majority and we may not all be lovable, but we do feel we are obeying a "higher law," and we know we are following in the footsteps of our Quaker ancestors.

---

[8] The Mexican-American War (1846-48) expanded the United States in the south. Many have regarded this war as an unjust, imperialist act of aggression on the part of the U.S.

[9] The hunchbacked Quaker Benjamin Lay, an early abolitionist pamphleteer, committed this act in 1738 at the Pennsylvania Yearly Meeting. He did so in frustration over Friends' slowness to free their own slaves. In reality, the "blood" was probably berry juice.

[10] The Milhouses were a Quaker family who came to America from Ireland. President Richard M. Nixon, against whose policies the 1969 Moratoriam was organized, was a Milhous on his mother's side.

[11] The Fugitive Slave Law made it a crime to assist escaped slaves even in states where slavery was illegal.

Quakers in American Literature

Given their impact upon the American conscience, it is not surprising that the Quakers have found their way into American poetry, storytelling, and legend. The following segments are representations of Quakerism in American literature. Two of the pieces are by non-Friends; the other two are by important Quaker writers.

Hawthorne on Quakerism

A descendent of New England Puritans, the nineteenth-century author Nathaniel Hawthorne was haunted by the wrongs perpetrated by his ancestors. Among these, of course, was the severe persecution of early Quaker settlers in the New World. He dramatized this persecution in his story "The Gentle Boy." Always a skeptic concerning human nature, Hawthorne also harbored reservations about the Quakers and their relentless quest for inner truth.

In the following excerpt, Hawthorne portrays a Quaker woman who has been exiled to the wilderness. Her child has been taken away from her, and her husband has been publicly executed. She has returned from exile to confront her persecutors in a Puritan church. The preacher has just delivered a bitter sermon extolling the persecution of the Quakers.

Source: Nathaniel Hawthorne, *Tales and Sketches*, ed. Roy Harvey Pearce, New York: Library of America, 1982, pp. 118-20.

The muffled female, who had hitherto sat motionless in the front rank of the audience, now arose, and with slow, stately and unwavering step, ascended the pulpit stairs. The quaverings of incipient harmony were hushed, and the divine sat in speechless and almost terrified astonishment, while she undid the door, and stood up in the sacred desk from which his maledictions had just been thundered. She then divested herself of the cloak and hood, and appeared in a most singular array. A shapeless robe of sackcloth was girded about her waist with a knotted cord; her raven hair fell down upon her shoulders, and its blackness was defiled by pale streaks of ashes, which she had strewn upon her head. Her eyebrows, dark and strongly defined, added to the deathly whiteness of a countenance which, emaciated with want, and wild with enthusiasm and strange sorrows, retained no trace of earlier beauty. This figure stood gazing earnestly on the audience, and there was no sound, nor any movement, except a faint shudder in which every man observed in his neighbor, but was scarcely conscious of in himself. At length, when her fit of inspiration came, she spoke, for the first few moments, in a low voice, and not invariably distinct utterance. Her discourse gave evidence of an imagination hopelessly entangled with her reason; it was a vague and incomprehensible rhapsody, which, however, seemed to spread its own atmosphere round the hearer's soul, and to move his feelings by some influence unconnected with the words. As she proceeded, beautiful but shadowy images would sometimes be seen, like bright things moving in a turbid river; or a strong and singularly shaped idea leapt forth, and seized at once the understanding or the heart. But the course of her unearthly eloquence soon led her to the persecutions of her sect, and from thence the step was short to her own peculiar sorrows. She was naturally a woman of mighty passions, and hatred and revenge now wrapped themselves in the garb of piety; the character of her speech was changed, her images became distinct though wild, and her enunciations had an almost hellish bitterness.

"The Governor and his mighty men," she said, "have

gathered together, taking counsel among themselves and saying, 'What shall we do unto this people—even unto the people that have come into this land to put our iniquity to the blush?' And lo! the devil entereth into the council-chamber, like a lame man of low stature and gravely appareled, with a dark and twisted countenance, and a bright, downcast eye. And he standeth up among the rulers; yea, he goeth to and fro, whispering to each; and every man lends his ear, for his word is 'slay, slay!' But I say unto ye, Woe to them that slay! Woe to them that shed the blood of saints! Woe to them that have slain the husband, and cast forth the child, the tender infant, to wander homeless, and hungry, and cold, till he die; and have saved the mother alive, in the cruelty of their tender mercies! Woe to them in their life-time, cursed are they in the delight and pleasure of their hearts! Woe to them in their death hour, whether it come swiftly with blood and violence, or after long and lingering pain! Woe, in the dark house, in the rottenness of the grave, when the children's children shall revile the ashes of the fathers! Woe, woe, woe, at the judgment, when all the persecuted and all the slain in this bloody land, and the father, the mother, and the child, shall await them in a day that they cannot escape! Seed of the faith, seed of the faith, ye whose hearts are moving with a power that we know not, arise, wash your hands of this innocent blood! Lift your voices, chosen ones, cry aloud, and call down a woe and a judgment with me!"

Having thus given vent to a flood of malignity which she mistook for inspiration, the speaker was silent.

Quakerism in Moby-Dick

Herman Melville's 1851 masterpiece Moby-Dick *tells the story of Captain Ahab's quest for the white whale that crippled him. Although Melville himself was not a Quaker, his novel features several Quaker characters, including Starbuck, Ahab's mate aboard the* Pequod. *Starbuck is notable for his piety, humanity, and circumspection.*

Late in the novel, Starbuck realizes that Ahab's quest will surely lead to the destruction of the Pequod *and the deaths of all on board. This puts him in a familiar Quaker dilemma concerning the limits of pacifism. Should Starbuck kill Ahab, thereby saving himself and the crew? Or must Starbuck spare Ahab's life, even if many must die as a result? In the following excerpt, Starbuck soliloquizes outside the sleeping Ahab's cabin while holding a loaded musket.*

Source: Herman Melville, *Moby-Dick: or, The Whale*; intro. Andrew Delbanco, comment. Tom Quirk; New York: Penguin, 1992, pp. 559-60. (Ellipses indicate a deletion by the editor of this volume.)

"But shall this crazed old man be tamely suffered to drag a whole ship's company down to doom with him?—Yes, it would make him the wilful murderer of thirty men and more, if this ship comes to any deadly harm; and come to deadly harm, my soul swears this ship will, if Ahab have his way. If, then, he were this instant—put aside, that crime would not be his. Ha! is he muttering in his sleep? Yes, just there,—in there, he's sleeping. Sleeping? aye, but still alive, and soon awake again. I can't withstand thee, then, old man. Not reasoning; not remonstrance; not entreaty wilt thou hearken to; all this thou scornest. Flat obedience to thy own flat commands, this is all thou breathest. Aye, and say'st the men have vow'd thy vow; say'st all of us are Ahabs. Great God forbid!—But is there no other way? no lawful way?...I stand alone here upon an open sea, with two oceans and a whole continent between me and law.—Aye, aye, 'tis so.— Is heaven a murderer when its lightning strikes a would-be murderer in his bed, tindering sheets and skin together?—

And would I be a murderer, then, if" ——and slowly, stealthily, and half sideways looking, he placed the loaded musket's end against the door.

"On this level, Ahab's hammock swings within; his head this way. A touch, and Starbuck may survive to hug his wife and child again.—Oh Mary! Mary!—boy! boy! boy!—But if I wake thee not to death, old man, who can tell to what unsounded deeps Starbuck's body this day week may sink, with all the crew! Great God, where art thou? Shall I? shall I?——The wind has gone down and shifted, sir; the fore and main topsails are reefed and set; she heads her course."

"Stern all! Oh Moby Dick, I clutch thy heart at last!"

Such were the sounds that now came hurtling from out the old man's tormented sleep, as if Starbuck's voice had caused the long dumb dream to speak.

The yet levelled musket shook like a drunkard's arm against the panel; Starbuck seemed wrestling with an angel; but turning from the door, he placed the death-tube in its rack, and left the place.

Many readers of Moby-Dick *fail to notice that Captain Ahab himself is a Quaker. In Chapter 16, Melville proposes that Ahab's Quakerism contributes to his tragic stature: "[T]here are instances among them [Quakers] of men who, named with Scripture names...and in childhood naturally imbibing the stately dramatic thee and thou of the Quaker idiom...strangely blend with these unoutgrown peculiarities, a thousand bold dashes of character, not unworthy a Scandinavian sea-king, or a poetical Pagan Roman." (Herman Melville, op. cit., p. 82; ellipses indicate deletions by the editor of this volume.)*

In the following speech, Ahab replies to Starbuck's accusation that his search for Moby Dick is blasphemous. Countless Quakers have been accused of blasphemy and heresy because of their reliance on the Inward Light instead of scriptural and priestly authority. But has Ahab's inward searching, however idealistic and heroic, led him to the brink of madness?

Source: Herman Melville, *op. cit.*, p. 178.

"All visible objects, man, are but as pasteboard masks. But in each event—in the living act, the undoubted deed—there, some unknown but still reasoning thing puts forth the mouldings of its features from behind the unreasoning mask. If man will strike, strike through the mask! How can the prisoner reach outside except by thrusting through the wall? To me, the white whale is that wall, shoved near to me. Sometimes I think there's naught beyond. But 'tis enough. He tasks me; he heaps me; I see in him outrageous strength, with an inscrutable malice sinewing it. That inscrutable thing is chiefly what I hate; and be the white whale agent, or be the white whale principal, I will wreak that hate upon him. Talk not to me of blasphemy, man; I'd strike the sun if it insulted me. For could the sun do that, then could I do the other; since there is ever a sort of fair play herein, jealousy presiding over all creations. But not my master, man, is even that fair play. Who's over me? Truth hath no confines."

John Greenleaf Whittier

Quaker John Greenleaf Whittier was one of the most popular poets of the nineteenth century. Many of his poems deal with his religious beliefs. "First-Day Thoughts"[12] conveys the meditative state of mind induced by a Quaker silent meeting.

Source: John Greenleaf Whittier, *The Poetical Works of Whittier*, intro. Hyatt H. Waggoner, Boston: Houghton Mifflin, 1975, pp. 433-4. (Also found in Jessamyn West, ed., *The Quaker Reader*, New York: Viking Press, 1962, p. 300.)

In calm and cool and silence, once again
   I find my old accustomed place among
   My brethren, where, perchance, no human tongue
   Shall utter words; where never hymn is sung,
   Nor deep-toned organ blown, nor censer swung,
Nor dim light falling through the pictured pane!
There, syllabled by silence, let me hear
The still small voice which reached the prophet's ear;
Read in my heart a still diviner law
Than Israel's leader on his tables saw!
There let me strive with each besetting sin,
   Recall my wandering fancies, and restrain
   The sore disquiet of a restless brain;
   And, as the path of duty is made plain,
May grace be given that I may walk therein,
   Not like the hireling, for his selfish gain,
With backward glances and reluctant tread,
Making a merit of his coward dread,
   But, cheerful, in the light around me thrown,
   Walking as one to pleasant service led;
   Doing God's will as if it were my own,
Yet trusting not in mine, but in His strength alone!

---

[12] *First Day* is the traditional Quaker term for Sunday. Early Quakers considered the traditional names of the days (Sunday, Monday, Tuesday, etc.) to be unacceptably pagan.

Jessamyn West

Jessamyn West's 1945 novel The Friendly Persuasion *chronicles the life of the Birdwells, a Quaker family on the Indiana frontier during the Nineteenth Century. In one episode, the Birdwells' peaceful farm life is disrupted by news that John Morgan's Confederate troops seem poised to raid the nearby town of Vernon.*

The family patriarch Jess Birdwell is secure in the Quaker Peace Testimony and has no intention of fighting—not even if Morgan's men come right to his own farm. His wife Eliza, a Quaker minister, feels the same way. But their oldest son Joshua wants to join the home guard in Vernon. In the following passage, Jess gently tries to persuade his son not to fight.

Source: Jessamyn West, *The Friendly Persuasion*, New York: Harcourt, Brace Jovanovich, 1991, pp. 67-8. (Unbracketed ellipses are in West's text and do not indicate deletions; bracketed ellipses indicate a deletion on the part of the editor of this volume.)

"Thee knows, Josh," his father said, "dying's only half of it. Any of us here, I hope […] is ready to die for what he believes. If it's asked of us and can be turned to good account. I'm not for dying, willy-nilly, thee understands," Jess said, his big nose wrinkling at the bridge. "It's an awful final thing, and more often and not nobody's much discommoded by it, except thyself, but there are times when it's the only answer a man can give to certain questions. Then I'm for it. But thee's not been asked such a question, now, Josh. Thee can go out on the pike, and if thee can find John Morgan, die there in front of him by his own hand if thee can manage it, and nothing'll be decided. […] No, Josh, dying won't turn the trick. What thee'll be asked to do now—is kill."

The word hung in the air. A fly circled the table, loudly and slowly, and still the sound of the word was there…louder than the ugly humming. It hung in the air like an open wound. Kill. In the Quaker household the word was bare and stark. Bare as in Cain and Abel's time with none of the panoply of wars and regiments and campaigns to clothe it. Kill a man. Kill thy brother.

When Jess' arguments fail, the family reluctantly accepts Joshua's choice. In the following segment, he says good-bye to his mother.

Source: Jessamyn West, *op. cit.*, pp. 71-2.

"Good-bye, Joshua," his mother said, and then not a word about his coming home safe, only, "I hope thee doesn't have to kill anyone." Joshua shut his eyes for a minute. "If thee has to die that's thy own business and thee won't anyway unless it's the Lord's will—but, oh, son," Eliza said, "I hope thee don't have to kill."

Josh opened his eyes and smiled. That was just the right thing to say...the words he would've chosen for her. He patted his mother's shoulder. Sticking by her principles and not getting over-fond of the particular—even when it was her own son. Josh bent and kissed her.

Epilogue:
Quaker Divisions, Quaker Diversity

While still a child, the American poet Walt Whitman heard the great Quaker leader Elias Hicks give a sermon. The experience had a tremendous impact upon Whitman, and much later in life, he wrote an essay about Hicks. In it, he related how, during the 1820s, the elderly Hicks helped provoke a great separation among American Friends.

Source: Walt Whitman, *Complete Prose Works*, New York: D. Appleton, 1909, pp. 471-2. (Also found in Jessamyn West, ed., *The Quaker Reader*, New York: Viking Press, 1962, pp. 331-2.)

One who was present has since described to me the climax, at a meeting of Friends in Philadelphia crowded by a great attendance of both sexes, with Elias as principal speaker. In the course of his utterance or argument he made use of these words: "The blood of Christ—the blood of Christ—why, my friends, the actual blood of Christ in itself is no more effectual than the blood of bulls and goats—not a bit more—not a bit." At these words, after a momentary hush, commenced a great tumult. Hundreds rose to their feet....Canes were thump'd upon the floor. From all parts of the house angry mutterings. Some left the place, but more remain'd, with exclamations, flush'd faces and eyes. This was the definite utterance, the overt act, which led to the separation. Families diverg'd—even husbands and wives, parents and children, were separated.

Of course what Elias promulg'd spread a great commotion among the Friends. Sometimes when he presented himself to speak in the meeting, there would be opposition—this led to angry words, gestures, unseemly noises, recriminations. Elias, at such times, was deeply affected—the tears roll'd in streams down his cheeks—he silently waited the close of the dispute. "Let the Friend speak; let the Friend speak!" he would say when his supporters in the meeting tried to bluff off some violent orthodox person objecting to the new doctrinaire. But he never recanted.

In his startling pronouncements, Elias Hicks was responding to an evangelical trend in American Quakerism. An increasing priority was being placed on the authority of the Bible as an infallible source of truth. To Hicks, this was a rejection of the original Quaker doctrine of the Inward Light—the "quietist" tradition of searching in silence for the "still small voice" within.

Shockingly, Hicks even suggested that God might do well to take back the Bible, leaving people to find fresh inspiration in their own hearts. And as the above passage by Whitman suggests, Hicks also strongly objected to placing undue faith in the outward person of Jesus as opposed to the inward Spirit of Christ. George Fox and his seventeenth-century followers would have found much to sympathize with such ideas. But to Hicks' more evangelical-inclined contemporaries, his teachings were heresy, pure and simple.

Hicks and his followers were so determined and vehement that they created deep divisions in the Society of Friends. By the beginning of the Twentieth Century, the Society had split into three branches, each practicing, worshipping, and living separately from the others. Orthodox Friends were inclined to evangelical beliefs; Conservative Friends preserved the quietist traditions of early Quakerism; Hicksite Friends were remarkably open to new ideas in philosophy, science, and theology. As the century wore on, these divisions lost much of their significance. Today, they are seldom even thought of.

Quakers remain, however, a diverse lot. Walk into many American meetings today and you'll find the same uncanny silence that bemused young Benjamin Franklin upon his arrival in Philadelphia. Walk into other meetings and you'll hear hymns and a paid preacher delivering a prepared sermon. Today's American Quakers range from quietist to evangelical; politically liberal to conservative; morally tolerant to strict and puritanical.

Despite their differences, American Friends as a group have done incalculable good during a troubled and violent century. In the United States and internationally, they have taken active roles in such causes as education, civil rights, famine relief, political amnesty, health care, pacifism, and nuclear disarmament. In 1946, Quaker Emily Greene Balch (see Chapter 2) shared the Nobel Peace Prize with John R. Mott. In 1947, the American Friends Service Committee shared the Nobel with the Friends Service Council of Great Britain.

Such achievements would not be possible if American Quakers failed to maintain and acknowledge a common identity. As a society, they are sprawling, diverse, and decentralized, but through some miracle their center continues to hold. The quiet voice that summoned George Fox away from his shoemaking still whispers to American Quakers.

Suggested Further Reading

Bacon, Margaret Hope. *Mothers of Feminism: The Story of Quaker Women in America*. San Francisco: Harper & Row, 1986.

Barbour, Hugh and J. William Frost. *The Quakers*. New York: Greenwood Press, 1988.

Hansen, Ellen, ed. *The Underground Railroad: Life on the Road to Freedom*. Carlisle, MA: Discovery Enterprises, Ltd., 1995.

Maurer, Herrymon, ed. *The Pendle Hill Reader*. Introduction by Elton Trueblood. New York: Harper & Brothers, 1950.

Sawyer, Kem Knapp. *Lucretia Mott: Friend of Justice*. Foreword by Rosalynn Carter. Carlisle, MA: Discovery Enterprises, Ltd., Second Edition: 1998.

Vipont, Elfrida. *The Story of Quakerism Through Three Centuries*. Richmond, Indiana: Friends United Press, 1977.